DISCOVERING D

FLYING REPTILES

Jinny Johnson

SAUNDERS
BOOK COMPANY

Published by Saunders Book Company
27 Stewart Road, Collingwood, ON Canada L9Y 4M7

U.S. publication copyright © 2014 Smart Apple Media.
International copyright reserved in all countries.
No part of this book may be reproduced in any
form without written permission from the publisher.

Printed in the United States of America, at Corporate
Graphics in North Mankato, Minnesota.

Illustrated by Graham Rosewarne
Designed by Hel James
Edited by Mary-Jane Wilkins

Library of Congress Cataloging-in-Publication Data

Johnson, Jinny, 1949-
 Flying reptiles / Jinny Johnson.
     p. cm. -- (Discovering dinosaurs)
 Summary: "Gives scientific facts about a number of
flying dinosaur species"-- Provided by publisher.
 Audience: Grade 4 to 6.
 Includes index.
 ISBN 978-1-77092-162-7 (paperback)
1. Pterosauria--Juvenile literature. [1. Prehistoric
animals.] I. Title.
 QE862.P7J648 2014
 567.918--dc23
                            2013003432

Picture credit
Front cover Merlinul/Shutterstock

DAD0511
052013
9 8 7 6 5 4 3 2 1

Contents

Pterosaurs 4
Pteranodon 6
On the Move 8
Eudimorphodon 10
Dimorphodon 12
Rhamphorhynchus 14
Pterodactylus 16
Anhanguera 18
Dsungaripterus and Pterodaustro 20
Quetzalcoatlus 22
Words to Remember 24
Index 24

Pterosaurs

Flying reptiles were called **pterosaurs**, which means winged lizards. They were not dinosaurs, but they lived at the same time, LONG AGO.

Pterosaurs were the first vertebrates (animals with backbones) to take to the air.

Scientists divide the time when pterosaurs and dinosaurs lived into three periods: the Triassic, Jurassic, and Cretaceous. At the beginning of the Triassic period, all the world's land was joined. The land gradually split up into smaller areas to make the world we know today.

Triassic Period: 250–200 million years ago
Jurassic Period: 200–145 million years ago
Cretaceous Period: 145–65 million years ago

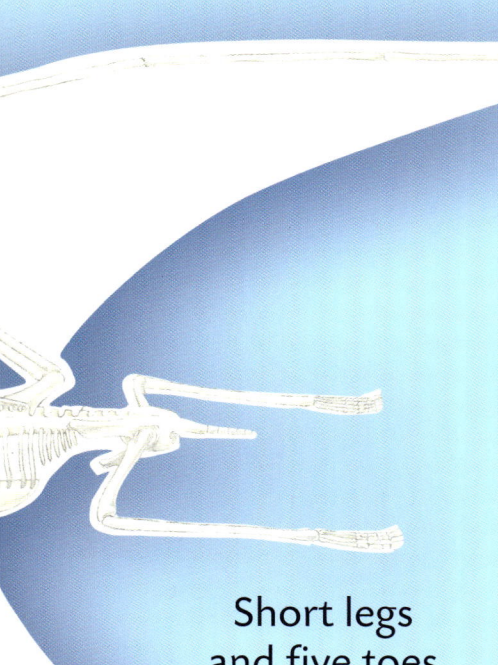

This is what a pterosaur looked like inside. Its wings were attached to the **bones** of the **arms** and **hands** and to the sides of the body.

Short legs and five toes on feet

Short fingers with sharp claws for walking or climbing

Long fourth finger held top of wing

**This is how you say pterosaur:
teh-rah-sore**

Pteranodon

This pterosaur had **HUGE** wings and could probably fly for hours as it hunted for food.

Pteranodon had a very large beak, but no teeth. The male had a large crest on its head that was longer than an adult person.

There weren't any people on Earth when pterosaurs were alive. The picture gives you an idea of how big a pterosaur was compared with a seven-year-old child.

PTEROSAUR FACTS
Wings: up to 23 feet (7 m) from tip to tip
Lived 86–73 million years ago

**Try saying this pterosaur's name:
Teh-ran-oh-don**

On the Move

People once thought that pterosaurs just glided through the air.

Now scientists think they could *flap* their wings and travel l o n g distances.

On the ground they probably walked on all fours, using the claws on their hands as well as their back feet.

> **PTEROSAUR FACTS**
> A pterosaur's bones were partly hollow and very light. This made it easier to lift itself into the air.

Eudimorphodon

This pterosaur had a short neck and a long bony tail.

Its beak was lined with lots of teeth tipped with several sharp points. These may have helped the pterosaur hold prey such as *slippery fish*.

Eudimorphodon probably perched on branches over water. When it spied a fish, it swooped down to seize it in its toothy beak.

PTEROSAUR FACTS
Wings: about
3 feet (1 m) from tip to tip
Lived 215–205 million years ago

**Try saying this pterosaur's name:
Yoo-dee-morf-oh-don**

Dimorphodon

A **big head** and **bulky beak** made this pterosaur look different from most others. The male's beak might have been brightly colored to help the pterosaur *attract* mates.

> **PTEROSAUR FACTS**
> Wings: up to 4 feet (1.2 m) from tip to tip
> Lived 195–190 million years ago

Dimorphodon had big clawed hands and feet and may have climbed trees to hunt for food.

Dimorphodon probably ate insects and other small creatures.

Rhamphorhynchus

Long-tailed Rhamphorhynchus soared over the sea like a huge seagull, searching for fish to eat.

When it spotted one, it swooped down and snapped up its prey with long teeth that jutted from its slender beak.

PTEROSAUR FACTS
Wings: about 3½ feet (1 m) from tip to tip
Lived 172–144 million years ago

At the end of this pterosaur's tail was a flap of skin. This might have helped it to balance as it flew.

Try saying this pterosaur's name: Ram-for-ink-us

Pterodactylus

Pterosaurs laid eggs and probably kept them warm by burying them in sand.

Young pterosaurs looked like tiny versions of their mom and dad. They had to find their own food right away, with no help.

Like all young pterosaurs, Pterodactylus probably ate insects and shellfish.

> **PTEROSAUR FACTS**
> Wings: up to 4 feet (1.2 m) from tip to tip
> Lived 180–144 million years ago

Try saying this pterosaur's name: Ter-oh-dak-ti-lus

Anhanguera

This huge pterosaur was bigger than the largest flying bird today—the *wandering albatross*.

Try saying this pterosaur's name: An-yahn-gwer-a

Anhanguera's large head was almost twice the length of its body. Its long jaws were lined with sharp teeth for catching fish.

> **PTEROSAUR FACTS**
> Wings: about 16 feet (5 m) from tip to tip
> Lived 110 million years ago

Anhanguera probably flew low over the sea to scoop up prey.

Dsungaripterus and Pterodaustro

Both these pterosaurs had special jaws suited to the type of food they ate.

Dsungaripterus

Dsungaripterus had long sharp jaws that curved upward at the tip. It probably used these to pry shellfish off rocks and then crushed them with its large flat teeth.

Try saying this pterosaur's name: Jung-gah-rip-ter-us

Dsungaripterus
Wings: about 13 feet (4 m) from tip to tip
Lived 144-98 million years ago

Pterodaustro

Try saying this pterosaur's name: Ter-oh-dow-strow

Pterodaustro's beak had 1,000 thin teeth that were like the bristles on a toothbrush. This pterosaur used its beak to filter tiny animals from water.

Pterodaustro
Wings: about 4 feet (1.2 m) from tip to tip
Lived 144–98 million years ago

Quetzalcoatlus

This **giant** was probably the largest flying creature that has ever lived. It had the biggest wings of any pterosaur and was probably an **expert flier**.

Even just its **beak** was three times longer than an adult human.

Quetzalcoatlus had no teeth. It may have caught fish but may also have fed on the bodies of dead dinosaurs.

> **PTEROSAUR FACTS**
> Wings: about 36 feet (11 m) from tip to tip
> Lived 70–65 million years ago

Try saying this pterosaur's name: Ket-zal-koe-at-lus

Words to Remember

crest
A bony shape on a pterosaur's head.

prey
Animals caught and killed by hunters such as pterosaurs.

reptile
An animal with a backbone and a scaly body. Dinosaurs were reptiles. Today's reptiles include lizards and snakes.

wandering albatross
The biggest flying bird today which has wings more than 11 feet (3.3 m) long from tip to tip.

Index

Anhanguera 18-19

beaks 6, 10, 11, 12, 14, 21, 22
bones 5, 9, 10

Dimorphodon 12-13
Dsungaripterus 20, 21

Eudimorphodon 10-11

prey 10, 14, 19, 24

Pteranodon 6-7
Pterodactylus 16-17
Pterodaustro 21

Quetzalcoatlus 22-23

Rhamphorhynchus 14-15

teeth 6, 10, 11, 14, 19, 20, 21, 23